WHEN YOU'RE A CHILD WHO'S different

WRITTEN BY

Abbey Luckett Benjamin

ILLUSTRATED BY

Michael Garriga

this book belongs to

When You See A Child Who's Different by Abbey Luckett Benjamin

Published by Benjamin Books

www.benjaminbooks.org

Cover and Illustrations by Michael Garriga

ISBN: 9798456318527

Printed in the United States of America

When you see a child who's different

WRITTEN BY
Abbey Luckett Benjamin

ILLUSTRATED BY
Michael Garriga

Hi everyone! My name is Avery Joy. I love dancing, loud music, and being outdoors. I have a brother named Tommy, and I love my mommy and daddy. I have a genetic disorder called ADSL deficiency; I have seizures and a button in my belly that I use for my food and drinks. I don't use words to speak, but if you take time to spend with me, I will communicate with you in different ways. I will laugh, smile, or hold your hand if I am happy. I may cry or scream if I am unhappy. I use my pink and white wheelchair to get me from place to place. I cannot use my legs, so my chair is able to take me so many places so that I can enjoy all things! I am not my diagnosis; I am much, much more. I hope you enjoy reading this book my mommy wrote. Always be inclusive to others, be kind, and love one another.

When you see a child who's different,
it's not polite to stare.

HOME 11 | 9 INNING | AWAY 11
BALL | STRIKE | OUT

They may have thick glasses…

or not have any hair.

There are children that move in wheelchairs
Purple, blue, and pink.

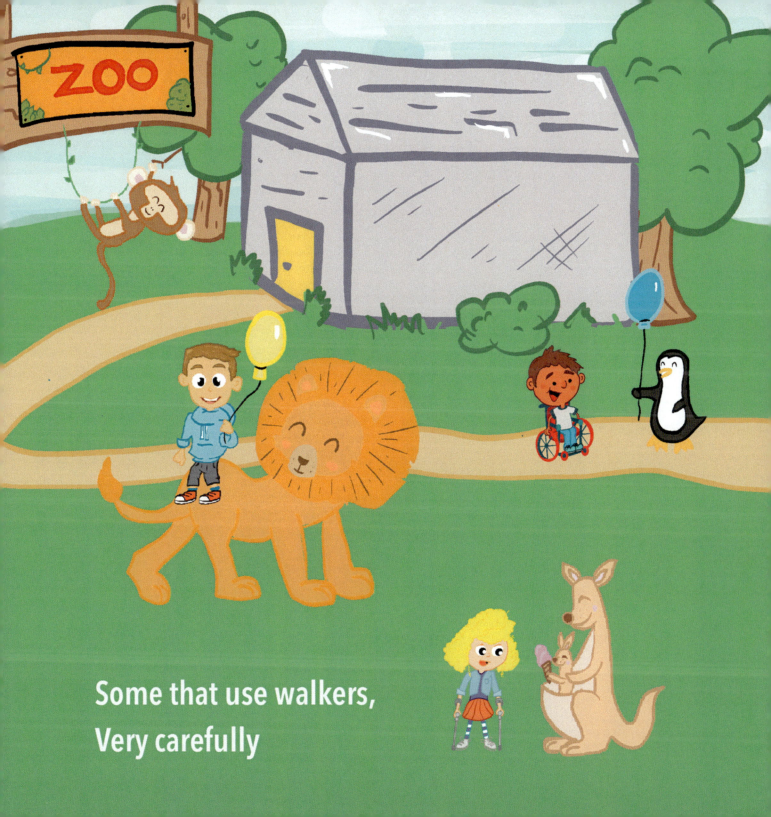

Some that use walkers,
Very carefully

Some go to lots of 'appointments' to try to help to walk,
There are even some 'appointments' to learn to eat and talk.

It's important to share a smile, a laugh, or a hug.
We do not know what one goes through,
And it's great to share the love.

So invite them to play, and hold the door.
Give them a hug and share your toys.

Include them in your games, your groups, your clubs.
New friends are great! Share the love.

Different can be special, and special can be fun.

God made us each so different, each and everyone.

Glossary

Epilepsy-Hi! My name is Avery Joy, and I have epilepsy. When I have a seizure, my legs get stiff, and my arms jerk in a rhythmic motion. Sometimes a seizure can look like I am staring into space. It is best not to be scared if you are with me when I have a seizure. Stay with me, call for an adult and try to help keep me safe.

Feeding Tube-I have a feeding tube. A feeding tube is just a tube in my belly that I use to get my nutrition. I have it because I have difficulty swallowing and eating.

ADSL Deficiency-I also have a diagnosis of ADSL deficiency. I am not able to use words to communicate, but if you talk to me, I have different ways of communicating. I can laugh and smile; I also scream or cry to let you know how I am feeling. Please talk to me; I can understand you even though I can't use words to talk back. I also use a wheelchair to move around. I use my wheelchair to go to school, take dance and go on many adventures.

Hearing-Impaired-My name is Annie, and I was born without the ability to hear anything. Hearing loss causes difficulty or inability to understand others when they are speaking to me, and it may be difficult for others to understand me when I speak. I got a cochlear implant when I was younger, and it helps me hear better. Some people who are hearing impaired use sign language to communicate with others.

Type 1 Diabetes –My name is Cade, and I have type one Diabetes. Having T1 Diabetes means my pancreas doesn't make insulin, or it makes very little insulin. Insulin is a hormone that helps blood sugar enter the cells in your body to be used for energy. I have a sensor on my body that tells me what my blood sugar is and a pod on my arm that gives me insulin when I need it. I love playing video games, swimming and playing football.

Alopecia-My name is Nora, and I have alopecia, which is another word for hair loss. It is different for each person. Some people with alopecia can have their hair grow back, while others do not. Please do not stare. I love to dance, sing and play.

Spina Bifida-My name is Amanda, and I have spina bifida. There are different types of spina bifida; it is when the spine and spinal cord doesn't form properly when I was in my mommy's belly. I use a walker,but some people with spina bifida use a wheelchair. I love country music, spending time with my sisters, and being outside.

Cerebral Palsy-My name is Cody, and I have Cerebral Palsy. It affects my body movement and muscle coordination. Symptoms of CP vary from person to person. I use a walker, but some kids with CP may use a wheelchair or not need any help walking at all. I enjoy swimming and spending time with my family.

Autism-My name is Franklin. I have Autism. I sometimes get easily overstimulated and m flap my arms by my side. This helps me feel calm when I am anxious. I do not enjoy loud noises and do not like to make eye contact when I am speaking to you. I love listening to music on my iPad and playing with my Tonka trucks. I would love for you to play with me sometime.

Abbey Luckett Benjamin is a self-published author who has set out on a mission to make the world a more inclusive place. Abbey lives in Mangham, Louisiana, and is a nurse, a dance teacher, and the mother to Tommy and Avery Joy. She has also written other books such as "In My Sissy's Wheelchair" and "Dance from the Heart." They are all available on Amazon. .

She hopes that after reading this book, the next time you see a child who looks or acts different from you, you will see that they aren't so different at all. Be Kind, Be Inclusive, and Love one another.

This book is dedicated to all those with disabilities, both seen and unseen, and both young and old.

Michael Garriga is a self-published illustrator and a compulsive doodler! Michael lives in Ruston, Louisiana, with his incredible wife Ali and their Cocker Spaniel Audrey Grace! When he is not traveling to magical lands in his head, he is working as a storyteller for the children and families at the Louisiana Methodist Children's Home.

As the great Walt Whitman said, "Be Curious, Not Judgemental."
Michael hopes that this book will change the lives of children with disabilities and teach kids and adults about being curious of others, not judgemental.

I dedicate this book to my love, my wife, Ali! Since I have set sail on this colorful journey, she has believed in me every step of the way and taught me to believe in myself. I couldn't do life without her, nor would I want to.
I also dedicate this book to those who wish to pursue their dreams but are scared to take that first step. You can do it!

There are **46** butterflies in this book! Can you find them all?

Different can be special, and special can be fun..

God made us each so different, each and everyone.

Made in the USA
Coppell, TX
19 March 2025

47297603R10017